More Than a Box of Crayons

poems by

Jenny Benjamin

Finishing Line Press
Georgetown, Kentucky

More Than a Box of Crayons

Copyright © 2018 by Jenny Benjamin
ISBN 978-1-63534-433-2 First Edition
All rights reserved under International and Pan-American Copyright Conventions. No part of this book may be reproduced in any manner whatsoever without written permission from the publisher, except in the case of brief quotations embodied in critical articles and reviews.

ACKNOWLEDGMENTS

Poems from this chapbook first appeared in the following:

"Grape Vines"—*Saluti di Spoleto*
"The Song of Sister Lucrezia"—*Chelsea*
"Shaharazad"—*Carquinez Poetry Review*
"Eight by Matisse"—*Diner*
"Haikus of a Sort"—*Fulcrum 6*
"Pink and Red Things" & "Grape Vines"—Selected for Watershed Reading Series, *Art + Literature Lab*
"Dappled Things"—read on WUWM's Lake Effect and published on the site's web page

Publisher: Leah Maines
Editor: Christen Kincaid
Cover Art and Design: Katherine Sandy, www.katesandydesigns.com
Author Photo: Stacy Kaat, www.stacykaat.com

Printed in the USA on acid-free paper.
Order online: www.finishinglinepress.com
　　　　　also available on Amazon.com

　　　　　　　Author inquiries and mail orders:
　　　　　　　　　Finishing Line Press
　　　　　　　　　　P. O. Box 1626
　　　　　　　　Georgetown, Kentucky 40324
　　　　　　　　　　　U. S. A.

Table of Contents

Collapsible Women 1

Yellow Things 3

Green Things 4

Haikus of a Sort 5

Purple Things 7

Silver Things 8

Grape Vines 9

Blue Things 11

Eight by Matisse 12

Pink and Red Things 17

Shaharazad 19

The Song of Sister Lucrezia 21

Dappled Things 22

For my Three Graces:
Sophia
Maggie
Ally Ruth

Collapsible Women

They have found no burning
trees in the far-off field
or in the lost purple skies
of their eyelids.

These women shadow
all their belongings and fear
what happens to their men,
but secretly they wish them dead.

Have you seen them squint on
half-cast days like their
thighs were not mothers or
cracked sides diminishing
in the light?

The only way to find them is
in the cool mud, philippic,
then apologetic for soiling,
ruining everything.

And the world means *everything*,
from hatching to thunderstorms.

They have secured their dead
children behind their eyes
without fail the babes, oiled and ready
for forgetting, will wail
and slip like otters into their minds.

As the day breaks, we see them packed
for anything, apatetic forms that come
their way or the way of the children
nested in deep beds of green ground cover.

They wait for the purchase of a mockingbird,
promised, along with pocket watches,
saved twine, and a foxhole for summer
tendernesses.

They will find a seashore or riverbed
to settle into with their chalky eggs
rattling with life.

Yellow Things

She wants to return to the sand,
grit and warmth in sunshine,
muck of brown wet after tides or rainfall.

The glass spilled it, tick-tocking our lives thus.

The underside of his body. The place of no time,
only butter stick and pancake morning of dreams,
the make-a-butter cheek of dandelion.
Daisy center.

Unknown nebula spreading its fire,
like he parts her she parts him, starburst,
these things that go cascading,
a fire spark, or landing party,
how the yellow paper of legal pads
or its miniature post-it taps memory,
the ticker tape, shaping our minds thus.

What is she writing?
A decree, poetry, novel,
or nothing, doodle pad lists her daughters gather
with their lives of here and there, or nowhere,
writes it on the yellow to make it stick.
We are sitting today, and nothing else,
she tells the daughters.
Merciful heaven, they comply.
They sit, their quiet eyes take in the yellow
of fading sun,
the burn of hours.

Green Things

Let the worm of hurt crawl through
the earth and bring fresh air.
The seed that drops will feel the whoosh
of breath and sprout and up the coming,

 YES,

life in green, smallest ever bursting bud
breaks through this OUCH I did not know you
could pain me so, but now a rib of growing,
twisting, reaching, up, up into dirt of layers
feeling.

Squash the never-no-not-now-we'll-see-of-never-seeing,
only here is

 GREEN,

the here it comes I can do this
I can be brave and keep on pushing even though
I've been told I am not beautiful,
an underling and weak,
a pushed-down thing.

Marvel, marvel this green coming,
breaking surface of the never-will,
busting up the earth and mortar,
weedy and surrounding.

Here she comes, I hear them say:
the green-eyed woman, once a girl,
her green shining.

Haikus of a Sort

Nothing makes me live
more in the moment than to
take an Italian train.

>Oily duck birth, shell
>a cracked, gleaming world, stained legs
>hazels, mice furrow.

Slowly, I become
Louisiana swamp land,
uncharted gators.

>Rotten splinter burn
>in the foxgloves and zinnias
>the leaves call home wet.

The poodles got dead.
Why did she tell us that?

>What vanishes?
>Water to the never here.
>Aunt Max in the black dirt.

Absurd cat banished
Tabby colors cold varnish
pennies coppered her mouth.

>   Pie-making is lost art.
>   The lich-gate needs something?
>   A little sin, good gin?

Sundays in the out
buildings court the octagons
of wire fences, wink.

>   Like a good-rumped horse
>   he trotted to the dust pile.
>   Hard rain and oatcake.

The swallows above,
some kind of tiny-lunged
machine. Grateful swoop.

>   Butter ripe and cashewed.
>   Go for the fatty side dish.
>   Who wants ham hock?

No moments go without.
She had legs like going on.

>   Again, I become
>   fallow field in a three crop
>   system. The watched pot.

Purple Things

Ground cover with green
and purple leaves like a
woman's wish. Toe touches
on grass tips. I want to sit down
in sunshine of butter yellow beams.
Not in royal purple, or papal purple,
but dirt purple meandering and
weedy with roots spreading into
earth oils and blood-root bottoms.
She'd been told to have fun now in
these middle years and loosen up.
Then the bombings came, of word rains,
barrage of hateful sleets masked in purple
monuments, the fortification of *right* and *just*.

When did this happen? These go-between
years, or purple-way-down to the bruises
and ruins, where the cloud doesn't protect,
but splotches everything, only slight rays
break through, and the constant count of every
day, where women wash and watch and gather
every damn thing throughout the day, keep
sentinel at the doors of homes, their fire eyes
warding off the bad ones.

Where is it safe?

Silver Things

Under the nail, peeling away no nickel wax, only glitter,
a child plays.

Now the woman can't remember what she is working on?
Not lab work, hospital needles, or chrome shining fucking
polished rooms and happy cartoon nursing smocks.
They take and test and remove and burn away.

Pray for better, pray for better.

"I am young, my mind focused and free," she writes on one
paper twist off the crayon, orange, apple, these real life things,
a completion happens on this day, a turn of events in the make-it, baby.

Going in the right direction this time, like the alien ship blasting
to another dimension, these super powers carrying the child.
And the woman doesn't die like appliances do.

Gleaming cast work on looms of drifting metals,
some say debris, some say free
space junk on the horizon of plenty.

Grape Vines

Across the green hill,
wedged between hedge posts,
concord grapes grew.
Purple heavens.

Each tired turn around the barn,
my face red, my arms tossed the air,
up, up, with my shoulders hiking
my heart into my throat.
My breath caught the waves of air
over the horizon on my Aunt Betty's farm.

I stopped at the hedge to study its gnarled paths,
as if it told me the map of the universe,
its origin and slow turns through time.
The grapes, delicate as bird eggs, drooped
and waited for me. My mother told me not
to eat the skin and seeds, but once the sweet
sank in my mouth, I swallowed hastily.
Grapes will sprout in my stomach, Mother said.
Fine, I thought, they'll nest next to the watermelon
patch, cherry trees.

Years later, my aunt sick.
Green bile and stomach acid.
All those moments to time just so.
Thrust the pail beneath her lips.
Catch the vomit.
Green heaven.

My aunt had the softest kisses,
a pink robe, a blue pillowcase
faded with washings and a landscape
of clouds cut the sky in two.

She was dying, and all I wanted
was to pick grapes off the vine.
Over time, I learned to spit the seeds.
I saw how they'd grow and die,
how the hedge post was both lovely and cruel.
I cannot go back in time, or read
the universe in the small hands of branches.
But girls, if you eat the seeds,
you will not die.

Blue Things

Of human feel and missing him,
the sky cast off into morning mist and waking slowly,
touch wood and wish.
Home is a mirage of light switch,
blinking and missing your child's smile,
hand hold and cornflower stillness
dotting wheat fields.
Tomorrow, she will continue
and tuck the sapphire treasure, hope,
between her legs, each crease he touches.

Mostly, I feel awarded, he says.

She collapses into *will this be?*
Will this be?
Does she like the fictions more than real?
Does she?
Bruises are more brown green purple
blossoms starting blue and this ache
to be pressed into,
curried with pushpins that say *maybe*.

Maybe.

Things have started from much less.

Let me earn the right to be with you, he says.

She wonders paradise moments down to his eye blinks.

Here and not here.

Open. Flicker.

Becoming.

Eight by Matisse

I.

What blue suffering
fell upon Icarus for his
exalted flight
into the heavens?

A flash of yellow—
furious yellow
into his eye
unable to swallow

his wings powerless
to hold his fingers
drumming the air,
as if struggling to reach

the button that snaps the picture.
A fall into the widening circle
of a bird diving to the red
fish in the water.
It appears and is gone again.

II.

I am a firm believer
in sleeping when you want.

Flop upon the table
like a plant overgrown,

untrimmed, misbehaving
as your too low-

cut of blouse kisses
your chest and dances

with the breeze that blows
from below your dress.

I am the vase placed on the tri-
pod in the room; I mark the still-

life with a three-footed center.
Beside the open window.

III.

Please cast that shadow for me
do it with ranunculi

for no other reason
than I cast nothing

because I am a painting
of a woman in a purple robe.

When I posed,
I did not know the moment
my shadow shrunk
to its own ending.

IV.

A Moorish screen hangs behind
the pale women staged in conversation.

The Shakespearean Moor breaks
a screen black to his rages.

The drama cries for answers
from an audience of generations.

But the questions keep descending,
never clutching the root of the tree
or the scream of the wind.

V.

Look to the horizon and see
the rooftops glide with golden
footsteps. The sun thunks
its brilliant lip upon them
and saddles up to the skyline
with a kiss. But there is no
tongue as in the bantering of love.

You move deeper into the mountain,
and I retain the water of the river,
though it is said it cannot be done.
What passage brings us to the green
beyond yesterday's water plashing
at our feet? Nothing.

You are in the mountain.
I cannot reach you there.
I do not try.

VI.

These things about the room hush to the final quiet in the mind:
a bowl of fruit, golden rod cut, bread rolls, wine untouched, lemons quiet
beside the dish of unshelled walnuts. A woman wears her hair gathered
on top her head; her collar crawls to her chin.
The picture window holds the hills in stillness. And on beyond
the shushed distance, through the window pane,
walks the company the woman held in the dark tin at the bottom
of her brain. It walks away while she grows thin, thinner.
A lonely, fetal thin becomes her, and her mind echoes din, din, din.
Repetition the final comfort.

VII.

She said: I was dancin' to a funky beat,
and I knocked over the Nasturtium.
Sorry 'bout that, but I just hadta swing.
You know how that goes."

"No, I don't. It's frozen now and covered
in broken glass."

"So are you. Look at the blood on your hands."

"Now it hurts," he said.

"I know, that's why I told you."

VIII.

The red fish in the tank
are seen so easily through
the transparent cylinder
filled with water.
They keep no secrets.
They have grown too fat
to live in such a small space.
They have been seen
eating one another.

Pink and Red Things

Blood. Gum. Tongue. Her sister said, years ago, after their disabled father
   had oral surgery,
"He'll be nauseated, weak, and bleeding from the gums."
Why years later the line comes to her often, a melody. "I'm sorry,"
she wants to say to the busy-busy parents of the parent gathering:
"I can't make it. I'm nauseated, weak, and bleeding from the gums."

Muscle, softness, the sound, a pulse of bacon frying in a pan, the
   heartbeat
background of her childhood. Her dad, three eggs, bacon, toast, each
   morning.
Coffee with a splash of cream. Housecoats and hair curlers, squishy pink,
   plastic pink
clipped. In the morning, the tears because her hair didn't turn out like the
   taste of
bubblegum-flavored balm. Pink boots, a washed-out hand-me-down red
   with Big Bird logo,
that lost their luster the days she forgot her shoes to change into.

"I'm sorry," she wants to say to her maybe date: "I can't make it. I'm
nauseated, weak, and bleeding from the gums."

Pink stick-out tongue. Pink wishes of shy and loud girls, becoming girls,
girls who simply are without trying to be something over there. That's the
call of wishes twirling or running in real-life shoes, not heels, run-able
shoes.

Pink journal, pink sweater, her favorite in middle age because it softens her.

Pink sadness of failure. Her girls look at her, like you are so wonderful-
awful-beautiful-harsh-meandering-centered, and she walks around on
Mother's Day wishing for pink roses and not saying so, just singing, "I'm
just a little black rain cloud, hovering next to the honey tree." And her girls
look at her with what-have-we-done? Not enough, not ever enough.

"I'm sorry. I cannot clean my gutters, sticky floor, and never-ever the floorboards because I'm nauseated, weak, and bleeding from the gums."

Pink candy wrappers, pink paper flowers, pink hearts drawn as valentines, as Mother's Day love.

Pink, the almost red. Her youngest writes in her own color poem, "Red is a blurst of blud when among green… sounds like a bird singing, feels like fire inside winter, is a flowr among the forest."

All the women here say red is childbirth, the crying, gaping of first breath and red tongue.

A push-start beginning. Girls born, taking pink in their fingertips and squish, squish, squishing, or turning it, swirls of their own making.

Shaharazad

The night stands colder than
her hands pressing against
the desert air. Her eyes look
to the stars for stories,

for the day to turn itself over
without delay or laziness.
The day's course matters

to her leonine gestures and thick
words. Her dramatic eye
squints and pauses.

Her life clings as an animal
near extinction, the mammoth
that lumbers through the dusk

air and clambers his hairy
body along a world
ready to dissolve.
And she holds ice in her hand,

waits for the night
to melt, for morning to
taste of salt. She waits

for his command that her
life can resist its own death
for one more day.
She could rebuild

the world and its words,
sunrises that truly
mean new life washed

orange and wide across
the horizon. Above the horizon
the stars dazzle themselves backward,
once more across the landscape

of sand. They dip into the darkness,
shine for her voice that carefully places
each word down with consideration.

Her words are worth the sky
and its arriving and vanishing,
its delicate strings tugging life up
and down no matter how many

small voices pray into the night.
And she understands her words
speak in the smallest of voices,
to a crowded universe of fading hearts.

The Song of Sister Lucrezia

Her song, the wide lung, extended beyond her slow life.
She posed incantations and sent them from her place
of motionlessness and waiting to fields of growing corn.
She sang for the boundaries of blue and orange
in a changing sky of illuminated spaces carefully planned.
The sky's mad glowing and delicate incisions slowly ran
as ink on paper.

Her voice picked its way through the trees outside,
moving unevenly, stepping slightly over underbrush
and rocks. It touched insects and moss without a thought,
but found no alleluia in the wandering. It returned to her
throat wanting more. She released into memorization
and counted beads until the sun went down and came up
again. She would begin again as if she had never started
singing, as if the clock never turned the new hour.

Her song was a fiery light from an exploding heaven.
Her brain smothered in it, her breast caught fire from it.
She touched the heat and withdrew from it because
it seemed a warm body waiting only for her.
She did taste His body and it was like honeycomb
at the break of dawn. The space it made between notes
stung for a word not spoken, uttered,
in sleep, when the lights were down.

The old trees outside cried for the wood carved into the chair
left alone, that waited for her to return, to sit and wait
for more time to decrease as she stared at the candle burning.
On the chair she muttered notes of songs to herself.
Even small they were exquisite, tapping out the crisscross
of thought. The sounds settled against the western wall
of the room in which she sat. They made a pool there,
disappearing into the quiet tremble of water.

Dappled Things

> *Glory be to God for dappled things…*
> *All things counter, original, spare, strange…*
> From "Pied Beauty" by Gerard Manley Hopkins

White and tawny, spotty belly
chocolate eyes outlined with sometimes
fear, sometimes courage to venture
out. Down the driveway, tail high,
ready for anything, except maybe,
no, not now, time to curl up, surrender,
give in and retreat, where the sun splays
strips of calling-to on a wood floor,
sawdust casts smoky fibers into the air.
The smell of work and tenderness.
She has adopted her first dog,
who would have told her this love
existed? The full heart opening wider to brown-white-
orange baby, dappled tummy for rolling
down into the dirty things that
announce the pup like an overture:
This song cannot be missed.
The dog-mom has spent her life
in search of purity.

That's why she writes poetry.

She notes ink splotches on white paper,
freckles, scraped shins, stretch marks,
psoriasis marks, rivulets of veins under
the skin, fingers typing fonts, paint smears,
blurred lights after eye drops,
whirls of smoke on the air.

She's read the dog is protecting
her when it rests on her feet.
Splotchy belly, warm and breathing,
on her toes, as she writes

nothing but da-da-da-da
hoping to hit the right notes this
time. Like love and the men
who have not made her feel so
since maybe the rugby player's
endless arms around her.
Silly, a dog, who rises with the
cough of the littlest daughter,
the mumbling of the middle one,
the worries of the oldest,
in the night, beside her.
She has a companion, finally,
to survey the perimeter,
test the locks,
watch for even the slightest
change in smell or breath.
Everything all right?

She marvels at the scattered toys
on the wrong carpeting;
she faked it was the one she picked
out in the store. Because who in her
right mind wouldn't recognize the
difference during installation?
Someone with too much
sight for other things,
like manners, pie making,
the correct use of pronouns and
commas.

How she loves the speckled dots
of dot to dots,

the page after page of scribbled
panda pictures from the littlest
daughter who started a panda club
at school, under the mom's unknown
signals to love all things roly-poly,
black and white masses of wonder,
the here and there of contrary colors,
taking the eyes ping-ponging,
the quiet of leaves flickering in the
breeze, splaying shadow and light
dances on the chalked-in hopscotch.

And the hoola-hoop sparkle, rain specks on
cracked cement, giraffe hugs,
adolescent pimples plus cover-up,
braced teeth, leaked-on sheets,
this go-between when she feels so lost,
a sun ray searching in bruised clouds,
then she tells the daughters to go out there
and flub. It shows that they are living.

She knows to embrace the clay shards
smudged with oil, all those broken pots,
and the things she is handed as a mother:
chewed gum, band aides with dried blood,
cupcake-crumb apple juice,
mottled flower-petal tangles of sweaters.

Looking down she sees dog paws,
cooling in puddles,
and then the making of step stones
on the patio that is Miss Havisham-ing weeds
between the cracks. Here she sits watching
crabapple blossoms twirl, listening
to the growly hum of beginnings.

Additional Acknowledgments

I would also like to thank my writing group, past and present, for feedback on these poems. An extra thanks for filling out questionnaires about their thoughts on abstract and concrete color relationships. Thank you, thank you WG: Colleen Harryman, Angela Sorby, Monica Maniaci, Catherine Koons Hubbard, Jennifer Dworschack-Kinter, Melissa Schoeffel, Liana Odrcic, and Kristin Bergeson Gasser.

Many thanks to my niece Kate Sandy for designing this cover and for Finishing Line Press for allowing this kind of cover input. And thank you, Sophia June, for rising before dawn one summer morning to take the lake shore picture of me that Kate used to make magic with the cover. Thank you, Maggie Marie and Ally Ruth, for sleeping like the angels you are.

Jenny Benjamin is the owner of her freelance writing business JB Communications, LLC. Over thirty of her poems have appeared in journals, including *DIAGRAM, Fulcrum, Chelsea,* and *the Crab Orchard Review*. Her first novel, *This Most Amazing*, was published in 2013 by Armida Books in Nicosia, Cyprus. Her chapbook, *Midway*, won second place in the 2017 No Chair Press contest and is forthcoming from No Chair Press in April 2018. She lives in Milwaukee, Wisconsin with her three daughters and dog.

www.ingramcontent.com/pod-product-compliance
Lightning Source LLC
LaVergne TN
LVHW041516070426
835507LV00012B/1618